Revision

1 **a)** Emma is at the swimming pool. Adriana is there too.
She has questions for Emma. What are Emma's answers?

> I live in Alphington. • I'm 12. • I'm Emma. •
> Yes, a brother. His name is Kevin. • I'm in year 7.

1 What's your name? _____

2 How old are you? _____

3 Where do you live? _____

4 What year are you in? _____

5 Do you have brothers and sisters? _____

b) AND YOU? What are your answers to Adriana's questions?

1 _____   4 _____

2 _____   5 _____

3 _____   _____

2 Sarah was in London, but now she's back in Exeter. She's writing an e-mail to Lucy
about what she and her family are doing later this evening.

go – cinema

visit – friend

play – football

stay – at home

Dear Lucy,

I'm back at home now. It's so boring here! Mum and dad are going to _____

this evening. Amy _____ .

Jake _____ .

And _____ .

Lots of love, Sarah

3 **a)** Tom is in Spain. Every day he goes to the swimming pool.
Pat, an English girl, is there too. Make Tom's and Pat's sentences.

I like sport. I like _____

_____

but I don't like_____.

I like animals. _____

_____

but I don't like_____.

b) AND YOU? Write what you like and don't like.
Write four sentences.

_____

_____

_____

4 **a)** Melanie and her family are on Green Hill Farm for two weeks.
Jamie is talking to (=redet gerade mit) Melanie about his school day.

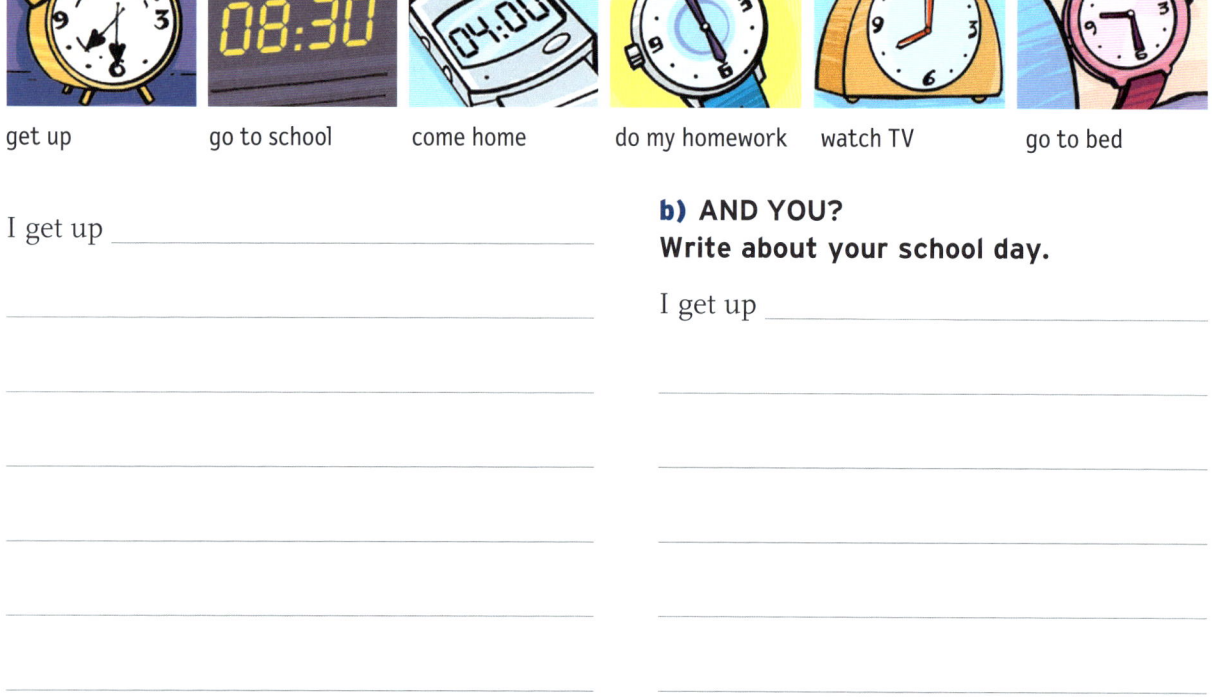

get up   go to school   come home   do my homework   watch TV   go to bed

I get up _____

_____

_____

_____

_____

b) AND YOU?
Write about your school day.

I get up _____

_____

_____

_____

_____

Unit 1
Back at school

1 Look at the pictures and finish the sentences.

1

2

3

4

5

6

1 _____ on this chair, please.

2 Do you like my new _____ ?

3 Can I use your _____, please?

4 Find a dictionary on the _____, please.

5 _____ the words on the board, please.

6 _____ the door, please.

▶ S. 11

2 Listen to Mr Rooney again and answer the questions. Put a ✔ in the right box.

1 Where do the pupils write the timetable? ☐ On the board. ☐ In their homework diaries.

2 When's class time? ☐ Every week. ☐ Every day.

3 What's the last lesson on Monday? ☐ Computers. ☐ Maths.

4 What's the first lesson on Tuesday? ☐ German. ☐ Art. ▶ S. 13

3 Finish the three lists.

➡ art • buddies • class teachers • geography • history • homework diary • parents • pupils • science • table • timetable • window

PEOPLE	CLASSROOM	SUBJECTS
_____	_____	_____
_____	_____	_____
_____	_____	_____
_____	_____	_____

▶ S. 13

Old friends and new friends

4 Finish the story. Use the sentences in the box.

➔ He thinks Tom doesn't have time for him now. • He's from Somalia and he likes football too. • He's alone in the playground. • Now Jamie is happy. • On Friday Tom and Tariq are making plans for the weekend. • Tariq has tickets for a football match on Saturday for everybody.

There's a new boy in class 8R.

1 *He's alone* _____ .

Tom talks to the new boy after the break. His name is Tariq.

2 _____

Tariq's dad plays for Exeter City.

3 *On Friday* _____ .

Jamie isn't happy.

4 _____

But in the evening Tom talks to Jamie on the phone.

5 _____

_____

6 _____

▸ S. 15

5 Read Jamie's e-mail to his grandma. Six things are wrong.
Underline (= *Unterstreiche*) them and write the right words.

Dear Grandma,

We're back at school. I'm in class 8A now. Our French teacher is Mr Rooney.
There's a new boy in our class. His name is Tariq. He's from Birmingham. He's a football fan.
His brother plays for Exeter City. Tariq has some tickets for a badminton match in two weeks.
Exeter City is playing. I'm very happy now!
Bye, Jamie

1 _____   3 _____   5 _____

2 _____   4 _____   6 _____

▸ S. 15

6 Mandy and Sandy

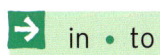 in • to

Mandy is _____ class 8C. Mandy is new _____ London.

She moved _____ London _____ July. Next weekend she's

going _____ the cinema with her new friend Sandy.

After the film they want _____ have a big ice cream.

▶ S. 16

7 Which subjects are they?

1 _____ 2 _____ 3 _____ 4 _____

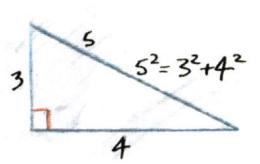   

5 _____ 6 _____ 7 _____ 8 _____

▶ S. 16

8 Write seven sentences about your favourite day of the week at school.
The words in the box can help you.

- My favourite day of the week is …
- My first lesson is … with Mr/Mrs/Ms …
- After that I have …
- The next lesson is …

- Then it's break.
- After the break I have …
- At … o'clock I go home.

_____

_____

_____

_____

_____

_____

▶ S. 16

5

five

9 Read the text and answer the three questions.

> *Judo club*
> *Our first meeting this year is on Monday, September 18th at 4.15 in the gym. Please come in tracksuit and trainers. This is a beginners' class so you don't need any experience.*
>
> *John Barker (sports teacher)*

a) Find *meeting* in the text. Which German word is right here? Put a ✔.

meeting ['miːtɪŋ]:

1 Begegnung ☐ 2 Besprechung ☐ 3 Treffen ☐

b) Find *trainers* in the text. Which German word is right here? Put a ✔.

trainers ['treɪnəz]:

1 Dompteure ☐ 2 Trainer ☐ 3 Turnschuhe ☐

c) Find *experience* in the text. Which German word is right here? Put a ✔.

experience [ɪk'spɪərɪəns]:

1 Erfahrung ☐ 2 Erlebnis ☐ 3 Praxis ☐ ▸ S. 17

10 Find the English words in the text for these German words.

1 Schlagzeug

[drʌmz] _____

2 vielleicht, möglicherweise

[pə'hæps] _____

3 Konzert, Auftritt

[pə'fɔːməns] _____

School Band

Do you like music? Do you play the guitar, drums or can you sing? Perhaps you're the right person for our band. Our first performance is at the school disco in November. Come and meet us next Friday, September 24th at 1 pm in the music room. See you there!

Chris, Lina, Saleem (Year 10)

▸ S. 17

6

six

11 **Make sentences with *Don't* ... The words in the box can help you.**

1 *Don't run*, please. It's dangerous.

2 *Don't* _____ now, please. We're doing a test.

3 _____ the door, please. Mike isn't here.

4 _____ your homework, please. I want it tomorrow.

5 _____ home late. There's a new programme on TV.

6 _____ on this chair. It's dirty.

• close
• come
• forget
• ~~run~~
• sit
• talk

▶ S. 18

12 **Make a dialogue.**
Put the sentences in the right order.

• At home.
• Chris, can I borrow a pen, please?
• Oh, OK. Where's your pencil case?
• OK, here you are.
• Thanks. And can I borrow your ruler too?

1 AMIR _____

2 CHRIS _____

3 AMIR _____

4 CHRIS _____

5 AMIR _____

▶ S. 19

13 **Say it in German.**

1 The holidays are over. _____

2 Close the window, please. _____

3 What's your favourite subject? _____

4 Can I borrow your dictionary? _____

5 Let's go to the playground. _____

6 Hurry up, you're late. _____

_____

▶ S. 19

7

seven

CHECKPOINT

Present progressive

Trage hier den Checkpoint aus dem Schülerbuch (Seite 21) ein und schreibe deine eigenen Beispielsätze auf.

Wenn du sagst, _____ ,

enden die Verben (z.B. *talk, read*) auf: _____ .

Meine Beispielsätze:

_____

_____

► S. 21

14 **Match the sentences with the pictures.**

→ I'm waiting for the bus. • She's watching a quiz show. • He's feeling tired. • They're reading a magazine. • You aren't looking! • We're doing a test now.

► S. 21

15 **What are the people doing?**
Finish the sentences. Use the words in the box.

→ having (2x) • listening • playing • reading • running

1 She's _____ an ice cream.
2 They're _____ to music.
3 You're _____ too fast for me.

4 He's _____ badminton.
5 I'm _____ a music magazine.
6 We're _____ breakfast.

► S. 21

16 **Tom is talking to Jamie on the phone. Finish the dialogue.**

JAMIE Hello.

TOM Hi, Jamie. It's Tom. What are you doing?

JAMIE I _____ (do) my homework.

And what are you doing?

TOM I _____ (watch) TV.

JAMIE Is your brother Josh at home?

TOM Yes, he _____ (stay) in Exeter for the weekend. It's mum's birthday today.

JAMIE Oh, that's great! What are you doing for her birthday?

TOM Josh _____ (make) a cake now. And dad and Sam _____ (help).

JAMIE Cool, can I come and help too?

▶ S. 21

17 **That's wrong! Look at the pictures and read the sentences.**
Then write what's wrong and what's right.

She's listening to her teacher. – That's wrong!

She _____ to her teacher.

She's _____ best friend.

"I'm eating a sandwich."   – That's wrong!

You _____ a sandwich.

_____

He's sitting on a chair. – That's wrong!

He _____ on a chair.

_____

They're buying a cake. – That's wrong!

They _____ a cake.

_____

▶ S. 21

1 **Make five more words. Draw lines** (= *Linien*).

class	exercise	football	homework	pencil	town
centre	book	case	diary	match	teacher

2 **Which word isn't right? Circle** (= *Umkreise*) **it.**

1 cupboard – door – shelf – uniform – window

4 English – maths – history – lunch – science

2 football – hockey – judo – rubber – rugby

5 afternoon – brochure – evening – morning

3 buddy – fan – friend – playground – teacher

6 laugh – meet – say – speak – shout

3 **Make sentences for the pictures.**

1 *Don't draw pictures on the board, please.*

2 _____ in the classroom, please.

3 _____

4 _____

4 **What can you say? Finish the sentences.**

1 Can I borrow your ruler, please?   – Sorry. I _____ *(use)* it.

2 Don't eat in the classroom, please! – I _____ *(not, eat)*.

3 Let's go to my house after school. – Sorry. I _____ *(meet)* my mother after school.

4 Are the boys OK?   – Yes, they are. But they _____ *(feel)* tired.

▶ Auf der Seite 65 findest du die Lösungen.

Unit 2

From Germany to England

1 **How do people go to England?**

1 They go by _____.

2 They go _____.

3 They go _____.

4 They go _____.

5 They go _____.

6 And some people _____!

► S. 22

2 **Listen to the three people again. One thing is wrong in every picture.**
Circle (= *Umkreise*) the wrong word.

1 bikes/car/tunnel

2 girl/book/train

3 Exeter Airport/Frankfurt/ woman

► S. 22

3 **TV Quiz! Can you answer these questions?**

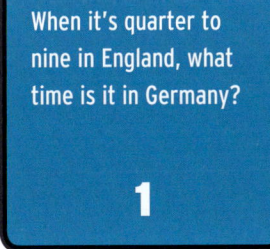

When it's quarter to nine in England, what time is it in Germany?	Do people in England drive on the left or on the right?	Nadja: "I live about one mile from my school". – Does Nadja live in Germany or in England?	Where can people drive faster – in Germany or in England?
1	**2**	**3**	**4**

1 It's _____.

2 People _____.

3 Nadja _____.

4 People _____.

► S. 23

4 a) From Krefeld to Exeter. Which sentences are wrong? Put a **X**.
Which sentences are right? Put a **✔**.

1 Jutta is Tom's sister. ☐

2 Jutta goes to England by train. ☐

3 Jutta goes to England on Sunday morning. ☐

4 The plane ticket is cheaper than the train ticket. ☐

5 Jutta's plane goes to Heathrow Airport. ☐

6 Exeter Airport is a big airport. ☐

b) Correct (= *Korrigiere*) the wrong sentences from part a).

A *Jutta is Tom's cousin.*   C _____

B _____   D _____

▶ S. 24

12

twelve

5 Listen to Tom and his mum. Put the pictures in the right order: 1, 2 and 3.

▶ S. 24

6 The youth club is planning a trip. Read the poster first.
Then read the questions and underline (= *unterstreiche*)
the answers in the text. Use the right colours.

1 What time do they leave? (Use blue!)

2 How do they go to Exeter? (Use green!)

3 How many places do they have on the bus? (Use red!)

4 What do they want to visit? (Use brown!)

5 What to they want to do on the River Exe? (Use yellow!)

6 Where do they have the picnic? (Use black!)   ▶ S. 25

Trip to Exeter

We're leaving at 10 o'clock in the morning.

We're going by bus. There are 20 places

on the bus. We want to

– visit the exciting Exeter Underground

   passages

– go canoeing on the River Exe

– have a picnic in the park and play games.

Come with us and have fun!

Exciting Exeter?

7 **a)** Put the sentences in the right order. Put 1–8 in the white boxes.

Jutta said, "I want to do something more exciting."

Jutta was happy. "Thanks, Tom," she said. "That was too exciting!"

Jutta was frightened in the small tunnel. "Help me!" she said.

Then they went to the shops.

They went to the River Exe.

Tom helped her. "Think of a big field," he said.

Tom went to the Underground Passages with Jutta.

Tom, Tom's mum and Jutta were in Exeter.

4	i
	g
6	i
	c
	x
	n
	t
1	e

b) Put the letters in a) in the right order.
Jutta finds Exeter very ...

1	2	3	4	5	6	7	8
e			i		i		

▶ S. 27

8 What does Jutta think? Write five sentences.

Jutta/She thinks	the River Exe tea swimming in the sea CDs in England the shops in Exeter	is isn't are aren't	expensive. very exciting. the worst drink in the world. very good. very small.

1 _____

2 _____

3 _____

_____

4 _____

5 _____

_____

▶ S. 27

WORDPOWER

9 a) What are the words? Write them.

			10				
	1	s					
	2	G					
	3	a					
	4	w					
	5	h					
	6	t					
	7	c					
8	c						
	9	l					

1 You can go to Britain by plane or **s**...

2 I don't live in Spain, I live in **G**...

3 Heathrow is an **a**...

4 Tea is the best drink in the **w**...

5 Sixty minutes is an **h**...

6 There's a **t**... to England.

7 You can sit down and drink tea or coffee in a **c**...

8 Your mother's brother's son is your **c**...

9 People in Britain drive on the **l**...

b) What's word 10? _____   ▶ S. 28

10 Fill in the missing words.   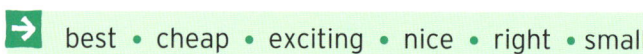 best • cheap • exciting • nice • right • small

Stop! It's not on the left. It's on the _____!

Cola? Big or _____?

It isn't boring. I think it's _____!

The worst music in the world? It's the _____ music in the world!

It's very expensive. I want something _____.

You think it's terrible? I think it's _____!

▶ S. 28

11 These people are in Germany, but they can't speak German. Help them.

A cup of coffee, please.

I'd like a bus ticket to Düsseldorf, please.

Is the Hotel Eden near here?

1 Sie möchte _____.

2 Er _____

3 _____

►S. 29

12 Help these people.

I'd like a bus ticket to the airport, please.

1 YOU

_____

_____

Can you help me, please? Do you know where the nearest bank is?

2 YOU

_____

_____

We'd like some milk, please.

3 YOU

_____

_____

Can I borrow your pen, please?

4 YOU

_____

_____

►S. 29

15

fifteen

13 **Read the dialogue and make the right sentences.**

ROBERT *This is / There's* Sophie, Ms Meral.

MS MERAL Nice to *meet you / listen to you*, Sophie.

SOPHIE Nice to *meet you / listen to you* too.

MS MERAL Is this your first *day / holiday* at our school?

SOPHIE No, I was here *yesterday / on Sunday* too.

MS MERAL What do you *think of / read about* school in Germany?

SOPHIE Well, it's *OK / terrible* but I think my school in England is better. We go to school later than in Germany. I can sleep longer every *morning / afternoon*.

▶ S. 30

14 **Make Maria's answers.**
Put the words in the right order.

1 in the world! – I think – it's the worst – CD

2 think – I – wrong. – you're /
is – Sugarcubes – the – band. – best

3 great. – I – it's – think

4 nicer than – think – Yes, – it's – our last book. – I

BINA What do you think of my new *Take Seven* CD?

1 MARIA _____

BINA It's better than your new *Sugarcubes* CD.

2 MARIA _____

BINA Well, what do you think of the new film *Communicator 5*?

3 MARIA _____

BINA Well, I think it's the most boring film this year! Do you like the new book we're reading at school?

4 MARIA _____

BINA You're right.

▶ S. 30

15 **Annina is staying with the Agarwals. What's Annina saying?**
Make the dialogue.

> • Yes, everybody is very nice.
> • Can I have a glass of water, please?
> • Yes, thank you.
> • No, I don't. But I miss my best friend.

MRS AGARWAL Is the breakfast OK?

ANNINA _____

ANNINA _____

MRS AGARWAL Yes, of course.

MRS AGARWAL Do you like it here?

ANNINA _____

MRS AGARWAL Do you miss your family?

ANNINA _____

▶ S. 31

16 **Say it in German.**

1 Lots of people go to England by ship.

_____

2 The plane ticket was cheap.

_____

3 How are you feeling now?

_____

4 I'm frightened.

_____

5 Nice to meet you.

_____

6 I'd like a hamburger, please.

_____

▶ S. 31

Vergleiche

Trage hier den Checkpoint aus dem Schülerbuch (Seite 33) ein und schreibe deine eigenen Beispielsätze auf.

Bei _____ Adjektiven (z.B. *fast, cheap*) endet die Vergleichsform auf _____ oder

_____ . Bei _____ Adjektiven (z.B. *expensive, exciting*) bildest du die

Vergleichsform mit _____ oder _____ .

Einige Adjektive sind _____ und haben besondere Formen:

_____ .

Meine Beispielsätze:

_____

_____

_____

▶ S. 33

17 **Which sentences are right (✔)? Which sentences are wrong (✗)?**

1 Scotty is bigger than Fluffy. ☐

2 Scotty is older than Dotty. ☐

3 Scotty is cheaper than Fluffy. ☐

4 Dotty is younger than Fluffy. ☐

5 Fluffy is more dangerous than Scotty. ☐

6 Scotty is more expensive than Dotty. ☐

Dotty,
April 25th 2003
£ 350

Scotty,
June 20th 2000
£ 150

Fluffy,
December 9th 2002
£ 50

▶ S. 33

18 **Finish the sentences.**

➔ the best • the most important • the fastest • the longest

1 Heathrow airport is _____ airport in England.

2 The tunnel is _____ way to England for cars.

3 The Rhine is _____ river in Germany.

4 I think Arsenal is _____ football team in the world! ▶ S. 33

19 **a)** **What's right? Finish the sentences. Put in the missing words.**

1 A car is *faster (fast)* than a bike.

2 A town is _____ *(big)* than a village.

3 January is _____ *(cold)* than July.

4 A DVD is _____ *(expensive)* than a magazine.

5 CD players are _____ *(modern)* than phones.

b) **What do you think? Write sentences.**
Use the right form (=Form) of the word and *than*.

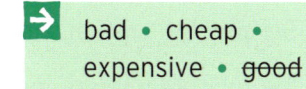

bad • cheap •
expensive • ~~good~~

1 I think a holiday on a farm is *better* _____ a holiday by the sea.

2 I think a TV is _____ a horse.

3 I think a quad is _____ a computer.

4 I think homework in Germany is _____ homework in England. ▸S. 33

▸S. 33

19

nineteen

20 **Look at the three cards about London,**
San Francisco and Berlin. Finish the sentences.

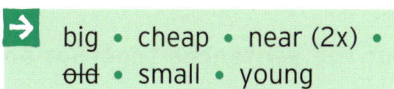

big • cheap • near (2x) •
~~old~~ • small • young

London (England)

How big?	1579 km²
How old?	1962 years
How near to the sea?	50 km
How much is a CD?	25 EUR

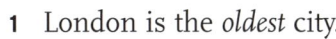
London   San Francisco   Berlin

San Francisco (USA)

How big?	120 km²
How old?	229 years
How near to the sea?	0 km
How much is a CD?	20 EUR

Berlin (Germany)

How big?	890 km²
How old?	768 years
How near to the sea?	230 km
How much is a CD?	22 EUR

1 London is the *oldest* city.

2 London is the _____ city.

3 London is _____ to the sea than Berlin.

4 San Francisco is the _____ city – it's only

229 years old.

5 San Francisco is the _____ city to the sea.

6 Berlin is big, but it's _____ than London.

7 A CD in Berlin is _____ than in London.

▸S. 33

1 **Make eight words.**

→ cous • kilo • mo • pas • sing • tun •
vis • wa

+

→ bile • er • in • itor • metre • nel •
sage • ter

1 _____ 3 _____ 5 _____ 7 _____

2 _____ 4 _____ 6 _____ 8 _____

2 **a) Which is the right sentence? Put a ✔.** 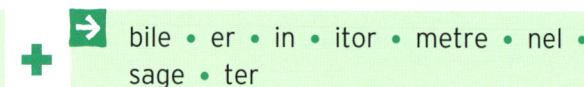 Do you know when this shop opens?

1 Sie möchte wissen, wann dieses Geschäft aufmacht. ☐

2 Sie möchte wissen, was im Geschäft verkauft wird. ☐

b) Which is the right sentence? Put a ✔. Can I have coffee instead of tea, please?

1 Er möchte statt Tee Kaffee haben. ☐

2 Er möchte statt Kaffee Tee haben. ☐

3 **Put the sentences together and make a dialogue. Draw lines** (= Linien)**.**

1 Nice to meet you, Annina.   It's great. I like English breakfasts.

2 What do you think of school here?   OK. But I miss my mum and dad.

3 Is the breakfast OK?   I like it. Everybody is very nice.

4 Do you want tea?   Nice to meet you too.

5 How are you feeling?   Can I have a glass of milk instead of tea?

4 **Make the questions.**
Use the right forms (=Formen)**.**

→ expensive (2x) • cheap (2x)

Tea 50p Cola 90p Milk 40p
Mineral Water 60p

1 What's _____ than tea?   – Mineral water and cola.

2 What's _____ than mineral water?   – Tea and milk.

3 What's the _____ drink?   – Cola.

4 What's the _____ drink?   – Milk.

▸ Auf den Seiten 65–66 findest du die Lösungen.

Hier kannst du darüber nachdenken, was du in den Units 1 und 2 schon alles gelernt hast.

Das kann ich!

Male die Kästchen aus. Leer bedeutet „das muss ich noch üben" [   ] , halb ausgemalt bedeutet „das kann ich mit Hilfe" [▨   ] und vollständig ausgemalt bedeutet „das kann ich bereits gut" [▨▨] .

Unit 1

Ich kann vier Sätze bilden, in denen ich jemanden auffordere, etwas zu tun, z.B. *Close the door, please.*
(Tipp: Schau dir die Übung 1 auf Seite 3 an.)

Ich kann sechs Schulfächer nennen.
(Tipp: Schau dir die Übung 7 auf Seite 5 an.)

Ich kann drei Sätze über meinen Schulalltag sagen, z.B. *My favourite day is ...*
(Tipp: Schau dir die Übung 8 auf Seite 5 an.)

Ich kann vier Sätze bilden, in denen ich jemanden bitte, etwas nicht zu tun, z.B. *Don't run, please.*
(Tipp: Schau dir die Übung 11 auf Seite 7 an.)

Ich kann um etwas bitten, z.B. um einen Bleistift oder ein Wörterbuch.
(Tipp: Schau dir die Übung 12 auf Seite 7 an.)

Ich kann in vier Sätzen sagen, was gerade passiert oder nicht passiert, z.B. *He's sitting on the table.*
(Tipp: Schau dir die Übungen 14–17 auf Seite 8–9 an.)

Meine schön gestaltete Arbeit. Der Titel meiner Arbeit für mein Portfolio lautet:

Unit 2

Ich kann drei Sachen nennen, die in England anders als in Deutschland sind.
(Tipp: Schau dir die Übung 3 auf Seite 11 an.)

Ich kann vier Sätze bilden, in denen ich meine Meinung äußere, z.B. *I think ...*
(Tipp: Schau dir die Übung 8 auf Seite 13 an.)

Ich kann jemanden vorstellen und begrüßen.
(Tipp: Schau dir die Übung 13 auf Seite 16 an.)

Ich kann vier Sätze bilden, in denen ich etwas vergleiche, z.B. *A car is faster than ...*
(Tipp: Schau dir die Übungen 17–20 auf Seite 18–19 an.)

Meine schön gestaltete Arbeit. Der Titel meiner Arbeit für mein Portfolio lautet:

Tipp: Du kannst auch deine Lehrerin / deinen Lehrer fragen, welche Fortschritte du im Englischunterricht gemacht hast.

PORTFOLIO

Das kann ich auch noch!

Ich kann vier Gegenstände in meinem Klassenzimmer nennen.
(Tipp: Schau dir Seite 11 im Schülerbuch 2 an.)

Ich kann fünf Verkehrsmittel nennen.
(Tipp: Schau dir die Übung 1 auf Seite 11 im Workbook 2 an.)

Meine Meinung

Units 1 und 2

Das fand ich besonders gut in Unit 1 und 2:

Folgende Aufgabe hat mir Spaß gemacht: Nr. _____ auf Seite _____ .

Folgende Aufgabe hat mir keinen großen Spaß gemacht: Nr. _____ auf Seite _____ .

Folgende Aufgabe konnte ich leicht lösen: Nr. _____ auf Seite _____ .

Bei folgender Aufgabe hatte ich Schwierigkeiten: Nr. _____ auf Seite _____ .

Lerntipp

Man kann die Bedeutung neuer Wörter besser behalten, wenn man sie sich in einem Satz einprägt.

a) Wähle sechs Vokabeln aus dem *Vocabulary*-Teil deines Schülerbuchs, bei denen du Schwierigkeiten hast, sie dir zu merken.

1 _____ 2 _____ 3 _____

4 _____ 5 _____ 6 _____

b) Nun formuliere mit jedem Wort einen sinnvollen Satz.

1 _____

2 _____

3 _____

4 _____

5 _____

6 _____

Unit 3

People and places

1 **Look at the people in the picture. What are their jobs?**

1 _____   3 _____   5 _____

2 _____   4 _____   6 _____

▸ S. 34

2 **Listen again to the four people and find the right answers. Draw lines** *(=Linien)*.

1 Who works late?

2 Who works on Saturday?

3 Who works in a park?

4 Who meets lots of people?

a The gardener.

b The cook.

c The shop assistant.

d The bus driver.

▸ S. 34

3 **Where do they work? Finish the sentences.**

1 David is a baggage handler. *He works at an airport.*

2 Gülei is a gardener. *She* _____.

3 Pavel is a cook. _____

4 Sandra is a teacher. _____

5 Sita is a security guard. _____

6 Tim is a farmer. _____

▸ S. 35

4 **What does Sarah say? Circle (= *Umkreise*) the right words.**

We moved to Exeter last *weekend/year*. But my parents weren't happy. They had no *house/jobs*.
Then my mum had *one/two* jobs, but she wasn't happy. Now she's a *bike courier/motorbike courier*
and she *is/isn't* very happy. In London my dad was a *cook/gardener*. In Exeter he got a job in a fast
food restaurant. The food isn't very nice and isn't very *expensive/healthy*. Dad *is/isn't* very happy.
He wants a new job.

▸ S. 36

5 **Where did Sarah's parents work?**

→ in a factory • in a fast food restaurant • in a restaurant • in a shop

1 First Mrs Johnson got a job _____. But she wasn't happy there.

2 Then she got a job _____. But the work was too hard.

3 Mr Johnson worked _____ in London. He was happy there.

4 In Exeter he works _____. It isn't his dream job.

▸ S. 36

6 **a) What things can you see in the picture?**

1 _____ 6 _____

2 _____ 7 _____

3 _____ 8 _____

4 _____ 9 _____

5 _____ 10 _____

b) Put the food and drink words into two groups: healthy and not healthy.

healthy: _____

not healthy: _____

▸ S. 37

A new project

7 **a)** Which sentences are right (✔)? Which are wrong (✗)?

1 Mr Johnson wanted to open a bookshop in Alphington. ☐

2 First he rented an old shop. ☐

3 Then he borrowed some tables and chairs. ☐

4 After four months his new restaurant was ready. ☐

5 On the first morning lots of people came in. ☐

6 Later Sarah came in with her friends. ☐

b) Correct (= *Korrigiere*) the wrong sentences.

A *Mr Johnson wanted to open a restaurant in Alphington.*

B _____

C _____

D _____

▶ S. 39

8 Read the text. There are five sentences missing.
Now read the five sentences in the boxes. Put them in the right places in the text.

Mr Johnson was unhappy with his job at the fast food restaurant.
☐E☐ Early on Saturday Mr Johnson and Sarah looked at lots of
restaurants in Exeter. ☐ Soon Mr Johnson had a new project:
a restaurant with healthy food. He rented a shop in Alphington.
He went to the bank and borrowed some money.

☐ In December his new restaurant, *The Sun*, was ready.
On the first morning the restaurant was very quiet. ☐ But at
lunchtime the door opened. Sarah and three of her school friends
came in. ☐

A Lots of people stopped in the street but nobody came in.

B Then the door opened again and more young people came in.

C Then he bought tables, chairs and things for the kitchen.

D The food was expensive and not very healthy.

E ~~Sarah had an idea: her dad could open his own restaurant.~~

▶ S. 39

9 **My family and their jobs. Write the missing words.**
Use *at, from, in* or *on*.

Hi, I'm Sunil. I'm thirteen and I'm _____ Exeter.

My mum works _____ a factory _____ Alphington.

My dad was a police officer. But he had a bad accident last year.

Now he can't work. He is _____ home and he sometimes

helps _____ a bookshop. My sister Anya works _____ Exeter Airport.

She's a security guard. My other sister, Natty, is a hairdresser _____ London.

She sometimes visits us _____ the weekend. My cousin Richard lives _____

Germany. He's _____ Stuttgart. _____ July I want to go there _____ holiday.

My grandma and my grandad are farmers. They live _____ a farm near Exeter.

I think that's cool. I want to be a farmer too – when I'm older. ▶ S. 40

10 **Circle (= Umkreise) the odd word out. Find one more word for each list.**

1 Monday – weekend – Thursday – Tuesday _____

2 milk – pizza – burger – chips _____

3 expensive – difficult – healthy – job _____

4 motorbike – bus – courier – train _____

5 mum – officer – cousin – brother _____

6 street – table – chair – cupboard _____

▶ S. 40

11 **Find the right order for these words.**

➡ 2003 • this morning • last month • last year • ~~now~~ • yesterday

PAST   PRESENT

2003 ▸ _____ ▸ _____ ▸ _____ ▸ _____ now

▶ S. 40

12 **a)** Look at the pictures and finish the story with the words from the box.

→ morning • boys • cafe • chair • had • happy • man • park • said • fifteen

1 Saturday morning

2

3

4 Fifteen minutes later

5

6

It was Saturday _____. Two boys were in a _____. An old _____

came in. He _____ a cup of tea. After _____ minutes the old man left.

Then the boys saw his mobile. It was on a _____. The _____ looked for

the old man. They followed the man to the _____. "Here's your mobile," they

_____. The man was very _____. "Thank you very much," he said.

b) Look at the pictures and write the story. The story in a) can help you.

1 Saturday afternoon

2

3

4 Ten minutes later

5

6

It was _____

_____

_____

_____

_____

▶ S. 41

COMMUNICATION

13 On the phone. Write the missing words. Use the words in the box.

→ how • what (2x) • where • who • why

Sandy

Hi, Sita. _____'s up ?

OK. I went to town.

Ben and Tim.

We went to *Cool Clothes* and then we saw a terrible accident!

Sorry, but I can't talk to you now.

Well, dad is back and I have to help him in the kitchen. See you tomorrow. Bye!

Sita

Hi. Oh, nothing. _____ was your day?

_____ was with you?

_____ were you?

Oh. _____ happened?

_____?

Oh, ... Bye.

▶ S. 42

28

twenty-eight

14 Talk about last Sunday. Look at the pictures and write five sentences.

The	boy children girl man woman	had helped played said watched

1 _____ TV.

2 _____ with her friend.

3 _____ his mother.

4 _____ "Sorry!".

5 _____ ice cream.

▶ S. 42

15 AND YOU? What happened at your weekend? Write two sentences.

Last weekend _____

_____

_____

▶ S. 42

16 **Which sentence is best? Put a** ✔**.**

1 ASHIA Hi, Samir. It's Ashia.

SAMIR ☐ What happened?

☐ Nice to meet you.

☐ Oh, hello.

2 ASHIA You weren't at the youth club today.

SAMIR ☐ Are you OK?

☐ I fell off my bike yesterday.

☐ Thanks for calling.

3 ASHIA Are you OK?

SAMIR ☐ No, I'm not. I hurt my foot.

☐ What about you?

☐ Yes, I had an accident.

4 ASHIA Can you go to school tomorrow?

SAMIR ☐ Yes, I can.

☐ OK, see you tomorrow.

☐ Bye. And thanks for calling.

▸ S. 43

17 **Say it in German. Read the e-mail and write the missing words in German.**

Dear Jutta,
Do you know what happened today? Our new maths teacher, Ms Justin, had an accident this morning.
She was late, so she had to ride her bike very fast. But the traffic lights near the school
were red. She stopped – and fell off her bike. She hurt her right arm.
She's going to be OK soon, but now she can't write. And we can't do the test tomorrow …
Bye,
Tom

_____

weißt du, _____? Unsere neue Mathelehrerin, Frau Justin,

hatte _____ einen Unfall. Sie hatte sich verspätet, _____

_____ .

Aber _____ in der Nähe der Schule schaltete auf rot. Sie hielt an –

_____ am rechten

_____ . Es wird ihr bald wieder besser gehen, _____

_____

_____ Tom

▸ S. 43

PRACTICE

18 **Emma is talking about her birthday last year. Which form of the verb is right?**

Well, it _____ *(is/was)* a Saturday.

We _____ *(went/go)* to the beach.

The sea _____ *(came/comes)* in and

our things _____ *(are/were)* in the water.

My dad _____ *(bought/buys)* new

T-shirts and everybody _____ *(has/had)* ice cream.

▶ S. 45

19 **Tom is talking to Tariq about his trip to the Underground Passages last month. Which is the right verb? Circle (=Umkreise) it.**

Jutta, my German cousin, *(came/crawled)* to Exeter and *(stayed/stopped)* with us. One day we

(opened/were) in Exeter with my mum. Jutta *(knew/wanted)* to do something exciting so we

(met/went) to the Underground Passages. We *(crawled/visited)* through the smallest tunnel but

Jutta *(fell/stopped)*. She *(made/was)* frightened. Then I *(had/saw)* an idea. "Think of a big field,"

I *(left/said)*. Jutta *(helped/thought)* of the fields at home in Germany and soon we *(were/worked)*

back in the bigger tunnel again.

▶ S. 45

20 **Sarah is talking about her father's restaurant. Finish the text.**

→ borrowed • bought • went • helped • ~~rented~~ • was

In November my dad *rented* a shop. Then he _____ to the bank

and _____ some money. He _____ lots of

tables and chairs and things for the kitchen. We all _____

at the weekend. In December the new restaurant _____ ready.

▶ S. 45

21 **Jamie is writing about what happened last year. Finish his text.**

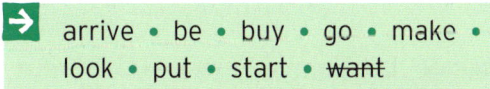

Last year in August my dad _____ (have) a terrible accident.

He _____ (fall) out of his tractor and _____ (hurt)

his legs. He was in hospital for many months.

Every morning, before school, I _____ (get up) early and

_____ (help) mum on the farm. After school I was very tired.

Every day dad _____ (sit) in the living room and _____ (watch)

TV. He wasn't very happy. In November my parents _____ (open) a farm shop. Lots of

people _____ (come) and _____ (buy) fruit and vegetables.

Mum _____ (say), "I think we're OK now." She was right.

▶ S. 45

31

thirty-one

22 **Murat's birthday party. Write the missing words. Use the right forms of the verbs in the box.**

→ arrive • be • buy • go • make • look • put • start • ~~want~~

It was Murat's birthday last weekend. He *wanted* to have a party. On Saturday morning he

_____ to the supermarket with his dad. There they _____ crisps, ice cream and

something to drink. At home Murat's big brother Wani _____ a cake. Murat _____

the party food on a table in his room. His mother _____ for good CDs. A four o'clock the

party _____. His friends _____ with lots of presents. It _____ a great party!

▶ S. 45

1 **What are the jobs?**

1 _____

2 _____

3 _____

4 _____

5 _____

6 _____

2 **Put in *was* or *were*.**

1 I _____ tired.

2 You _____ right.

3 There _____ no jobs in London.

4 It _____ her dream job.

3 **Finish the sentences. Use the simple past forms of the verbs in the box.**

1 He _____ no job and he was unhappy.

2 She _____ a salad roll for me.

3 I _____ you with your dad in a cafe.

4 She _____ to the bank and borrowed some money.

5 We _____ fish and chips for lunch.

6 They _____ at the new clothes shop yesterday.

➜
- go
- have (2x)
- look
- make
- see

4 **Make the dialogue. Pick the right words. Circle (= Umkreise) them.**

SARAH   Hi, Emma! How *was/were* your weekend?

EMMA   *Fine/Terrible.* I went to the *sports centre/cinema.* We *watched/bought* a great film.

Where/What about you?

SARAH   Oh, I fell off a *horse/chicken.*

EMMA   *That's nice! / Poor you!* Are you OK?

SARAH   *No, I'm not. / Yes, I am.* I hurt my arm. I can't go to school *yesterday/tomorrow.*

▶ Auf der Seite 66 findest du die Lösungen.

Unit 4
A weekend in Exeter

1 **a)** Listen again. What are the people talking about? Put the pictures in the right order. Put 1, 2, 3 and 4 in the boxes.

b) Listen and underline *(=unterstreiche)* the right word.

1 The boy has a friend in *Germany/Spain/England*.

2 The woman lives near a *bank/supermarket/post office*.

3 The woman needs *money/magazines/books* for her trip to America.

4 The two girls want to meet at *10/11/12* o'clock tomorrow. ▶ S. 46

2 **AND YOU?** What would you like to do in your town on Sundays? What wouldn't you like to do? Write six sentences. Use the words in the boxes or think of other words.

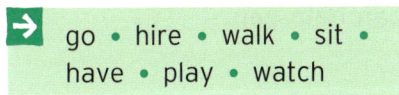 go • hire • walk • sit • have • play • watch

bikes • next to the river • in the park • football • shopping • sport • an ice cream • TV

1 *I'd like to* _____ .   4 *I wouldn't like to* _____ .

2 _____   5 _____

3 _____   6 _____

▶ S. 47

3 **Quiz:** What do you know about England and Germany? Answer the questions with *Yes, you can.* or *No, you can't.*

1 Can you use euros in England? _____

2 Can you use euros in Germany? _____

3 Can you go to the post office in Germany on Sundays? _____

4 Can you go shopping at some stores in England on Sundays? _____

▶ S. 47

4 **Look at the sentences. Put in the right names.**

→ Emma (2x) • Mrs Baker (2x) • Mr Baker • Sally

1 _____ needs some money.

2 _____ didn't win the lotto.

3 _____ wants to go to Exmouth.

4 _____ wants to go to London.

5 _____ is working for *Securex*.

6 _____ has time for Emma.

▶ S. 48

5 **What do Sally and Emma want to do at the weekend? Find the answer.**

Answer: _____

▶ S. 48

6 **What's missing in these adverts? The sentences in the box can help you.**

→ Do you need more money? • Swim in our pool! • Wear them today! •
And you don't want to go to a restaurant?

▶ S. 49

Did you pay for that?

7 **a)** **Sally is talking to her brother. What's she saying?**

> ➡ liked • looked • put • went

We _____ into Debenhams on Saturday.

We _____ at the T-shirts. Emma _____

a yellow T-shirt. I _____ it in my bag.

> ➡ fell • gave • ran • shouted • turned • were

Suddenly somebody _____ ,"Stop the two girls!"

It was a security guard. I _____ the bag to Emma and

ran towards the door. Emma _____ towards the door

too. I _____ left and she turned right. There

_____ steps and Emma _____ to the ground.

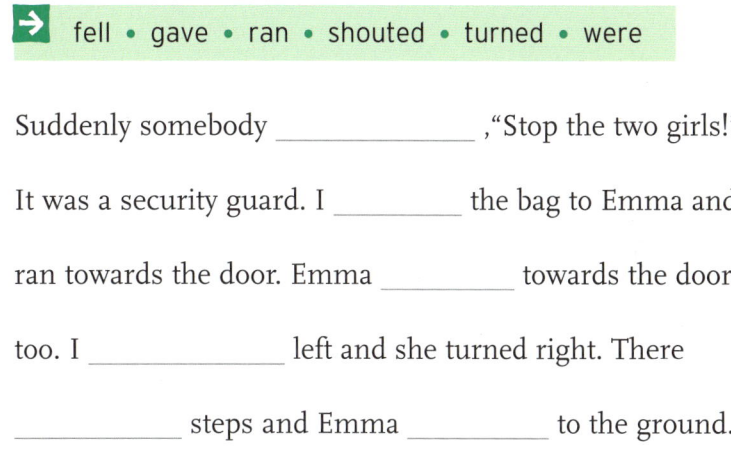

> ➡ said • talked • was • went

The security guard _____ Emma's mum! On

Saturday evening Emma and I _____ on the

phone. On Sunday we _____ to the department

store again and _____ sorry. It was terrible!

b) **Put the words in the right order and finish the sentences.**

1 *didn't pay / and / took / she / the clothes*

Sally was stupid, because _____.

2 *out of / she / Sally / the shop / followed*

Emma was stupid, because _____.

3 *a / daughter / her / shoplifter / was*

Emma's mum wasn't happy, because _____.

▶ S. 51

35

thirty-five

WORDPOWER

8 a) Write the verbs in the simple past.

→
1 feel
2 come
3 crawl
4 drink
5 hurt
6 buy
7 stop
8 hate

M M   S   S   I

b) What sentence did you find?

_____

► S. 52

9 Put the words in the right box. Think of more words.

→ adverts • banks • bikes • cafes • canoes • cars • chips • chocolate • department stores • newspapers • pizza • postcards

You eat				
You go to				
You hire				
You read				

► S. 52

10 Which verb is right? Underline (=Unterstreiche) it.

1 The man *borrowed / made / paid for* the tea.

2 The woman *pushed / put / sold* the newspaper on the table.

3 The boy *fell to / ran towards / moved to* the ground.

4 The girl *hired / took / wore* new jeans.

► S. 52

11 Nobody can read this police report. There's tea on it. Finish the text with the words in the box.

→ at • into (2x) • past • through • to • towards • with

REPORT

On March 14th, a young man came _____ the shop. He looked _____ a new camera. Suddenly he put the camera in his bag. He ran _____ the door. I followed him _____ the shop _____ all the other shoppers. He ran _____ Castle Street. I shouted, "Stop!" but he didn't stop. Suddenly he fell _____ the ground. I had him now. "OK, young man," I said. "You're coming _____ me."

▶ S. 53

12 Look at the pictures and write a report. Use verbs in the simple past. Exercise 11 can help you.

March 5th

Stop!

London Road

▶ S. 53

thirty-seven

13 **Write Marla's answers.**

➡ I bought this CD. • Well, it was OK. • We went shopping. • Yes, on Saturday afternoon.

ANYA   MARLA

Did you have a good weekend?   – _____

Did you meet your friends?   – _____

                                       _____

What did you do?   – _____

And what did you buy?   – _____

► S. 54

14 **Look at the pictures and the sentences in the box. Then answer the questions.**

➡ At eight o'clock. • I had a hamburger and cola with my friends. • I played basketball. •
No, I didn't. I went to bed early. • No, I didn't. We went to the sports centre. • ~~Yes, I did.~~

1 Did you have a nice weekend?      *Yes, I did.*

2 Did you go dancing?      _____
                                                                  _____

3 What did you do there?   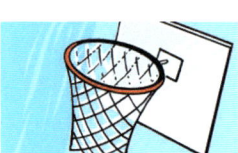   _____
                                                                  _____

4 What did you do then?      _____
                                                                  _____

5 When did you get home?      _____
                                                                  _____

6 Did you watch TV?      _____
                                                                  _____

► S. 54

15 **What did the Smith family do yesterday? Look at the pictures and write the answers.**

→ • Yes, he/she/they did.
• No, he/she/they didn't.

1 Did they have breakfast? _____

2 Did dad do the shopping? _____

3 Did Bina do her homework? _____

4 Did Amir and his friend hire a canoe? _____

5 Did grandma win the lotto? _____

6 Did the family have a party? _____

▶ S. 54

16 **Read the question. Two answers are right. Put a ✔.**

1 What did you do yesterday?

☐ I stayed at home. ☐ Yes, I did. ☐ Nothing.

2 Did you talk to your mum about the party?

☐ Yes, of course. ☐ Yes, I did. ☐ Yes, let's go.

3 Did you have a nice holiday?

☐ It was OK. ☐ No, she wasn't at home. ☐ No, I didn't.

4 Did you stay at Mike's house long?

☐ He was OK. ☐ No, I didn't. I left at eight. ☐ Not very long. ▶ S. 55

17 **Say it in German.**

1 The shop is open 24 hours a day. _____

2 Did you read this advert? _____

3 Did you have a good weekend? _____

_____

4 I'm sorry I'm late. _____

▶ S. 55

39

thirty-nine

PRACTICE

► S. 57

CHECKPOINT

Simple past

Trage hier den Checkpoint aus dem Schülerbuch (Seite 57) ein und schreibe deine eigenen Beispielsätze auf.

Bei _____ über die Vergangenheit verwendest du _____.

Wenn du sagen willst, was _____, verwendest du _____.

Meine Beispielsätze:

_____

_____

► S. 57

18 Emma's grandad wants to know about Emma's day at school. What are his questions?

GRANDAD

1 What / you / did / at school? / do _____

2 lessons / did / How many / have? / you _____

3 say? / What / the teachers / did _____

4 did / When / start? / break _____

5 after school? / did / Where / Kevin / go _____

► S. 57

19 Read the answers. Then make questions. Use *Did you ...* and the words from the box.

→ do your homework on Saturday • ~~go home after school~~ •
have a nice evening • watch TV in the afternoon

1 *Did you go home after school?*

No, I didn't. I met some friends in town.

2 _____

No, I didn't. I was in Exmouth all day.

3 _____

Yes, I did. The quiz show was great.

4 _____

Yes, I did. I went to the cinema with my friends.

► S. 57

20 Sophia isn't happy with Paul. Make the dialogue.

1 SOPHIA   Hey! You *didn't write* (not/write) an e-mail to me yesterday.

   PAUL   I'm sorry, but I *didn't work* (not/work) on the computer.

2 SOPHIA   Hey! You _____ (not/wait) for me after school.

   PAUL   I'm sorry, but I _____ (not/have) time.

3 SOPHIA   Hey! You _____ (not/show) me your homework.

   PAUL   I'm sorry, but I _____ (not/do) it.

4 SOPHIA   Hey! You _____ (not/say hello) to me yesterday.

   PAUL   I'm sorry, but I _____ (not/see) you.

5 SOPHIA   Hey! You _____ (not/go) to the cinema with me.

   PAUL   I'm sorry, but I _____ (not/want) to see the film.

6 SOPHIA   Hey! You _____ (not/take) me to the station.

   PAUL   I'm sorry, but my mum _____ (not/have) the car.　▸ S. 57

21 What did Emma do and what didn't Emma do in Debenhams?
Finish her sentences.

1 I met Sally in town. I _____ Sarah in town.

2 We went to Debenhams. We _____ to a cafe.

3 We looked at clothes. We _____ at CDs.

4 Sally took the yellow T-shirt. I _____ the T-shirt.

5 I turned right. Sally _____ right.

6 Mum followed me into Market Street. She _____ Sally.

7 We had to say sorry. Mum _____ to say sorry.　▸ S. 57

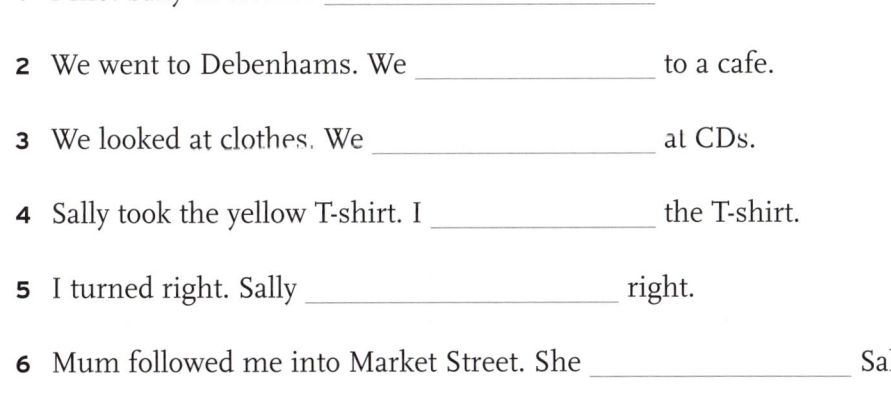

TEST YOURSELF

1 It's Monday afternoon. What would Ben like to do (✔)?
What wouldn't he like to do (✘)? Write four sentences.

→ go shopping (✘) • watch TV (✔) • eat an ice cream (✔) • play alone (✘)

BEN

1 *I wouldn't like* _____

2 _____

3 _____

4 _____

2 Make six words.

→ auto • girl • news • shop • some • week

+

→ end • friend • graph • lifter • paper • times

1 *autograph*

3 _____

5 _____

2 _____

4 _____

6 _____

3 What the Lees didn't do yesterday.

1 *go / shopping / Mr Lee / didn't* _____

2 *didn't / TV / Mrs Lee / watch* _____

3 *read / his / new / book / didn't / David* _____

4 In the evening dad is asking Josh questions about his day.
Look at the pictures and make the dialogue.

DAD

1 *Did you* go to the supermarket?

2 _____ grandma?

3 _____ homework?

4 _____ mum?

JOSH

No, I didn't.

Yes, _____.

_____

_____

▶ Auf der Seite 67 findest du die Lösungen.

Hier kannst du darüber nachdenken, was du in den Units 3 und 4 schon alles gelernt hast.

Das kann ich!

Male die Kästchen aus. Leer bedeutet „das muss ich noch üben" ☐ , halb ausgemalt bedeutet „das kann ich mit Hilfe" ▨ und vollständig ausgemalt bedeutet „das kann ich bereits gut" ▨ .

Unit 3

Ich kann sechs Berufe nennen.
(Tipp: Schau dir die Übung 1 auf Seite 23 an.)

Ich kann vier Sätze bilden, in denen ich sage, wo jemand arbeitet.
(Tipp: Schau dir die Übung 3 auf Seite 23 an.)

Ich kann vier gesunde Lebensmittel nennen.
(Tipp: Schau dir die Übung 6b auf Seite 24 an.)

Ich kann in zwei Sätzen sagen, was ich am Wochenende gemacht habe,
z.B. *I played ..., I went to ...*
(Tipp: Schau dir die Übung 15 auf Seite 28 an.)

Ich kann eine kurze Geschichte in fünf Sätzen nacherzählen.
(Tipp: Schau dir die Übungen 18−22 auf Seite 30−31 an.)

Meine schön gestaltete Arbeit. Der Titel meiner Arbeit für mein Portfolio lautet:

Unit 4

Ich kann vier Sätze bilden, in denen ich sage, was ich gern
oder nicht gern am Wochenende tun würde,
z.B. *I'd like to ...*
(Tipp: Schau dir die Übung 2 auf Seite 33 an.)

Ich kann fragen, ob jemand etwas getan hat,
z.B. *Did you ...?*
(Tipp: Schau dir die Übung 19 auf Seite 40 an.)

Ich kann sagen, was nicht geschehen ist,
z.B. *You didn't ...*
(Tipp: Schau dir die Übung 20 auf Seite 41 an.)

Ich kann mich für etwas entschuldigen.
(Tipp: Schau dir die Übung 20 auf Seite 41 an.)

Meine schön gestaltete Arbeit. Der Titel meiner Arbeit für mein Portfolio lautet:

Tipp: Du kannst auch deine Lehrerin / deinen Lehrer fragen,
welche Fortschritte du im Englischunterricht gemacht hast.

PORTFOLIO

Das kann ich auch noch!

Ich kann fünf Gebäude nennen, die es in einer Stadt gibt, z.B. *school*.
(Tipp: Schau dir Seite 35 im Schülerbuch 2 an.)

Ich kann fünf Aktivitäten nennen, die man am Wochenende tun kann.
(Tipp: Schau dir Seite 47 im Schülerbuch 2 an.)

So lerne ich Englisch!

In Units 3 und 4 habe ich folgende Schwierigkeiten gehabt:

.

Ich habe mir dann geholfen, indem ich

Ich wollte meine Lehrerin / meinen Lehrer noch zu folgenden Aufgaben / zu dem folgenden

Problem etwas fragen: .

In den nächsten Stunden würde ich gern Folgendes lernen:

.

Lerntipp

Um erfolgreich zum Gipfel zu kommen, muss man langsam gehen und Pausen einlegen. Man darf nicht gleich eine steile Kletterroute wählen, sonst wird man schnell müde und mutlos. Setze dir kleine Ziele!

Du hast gelernt, wie du mit einem neuen Text umgehen kannst. Hier sind die einzelnen Arbeitsschritte in der falschen Reihenfolge. Ordne sie.

[ ] Ich lese den Text noch einmal.

[ ] Ich schlage die schwierigen Wörter im *dictionary* nach.

[ ] Ich lese die Überschrift und überlege, worum es im Text geht.

[1] Wenn es ein Bild zum Text gibt, schaue ich es mir zuerst an.

[ ] Ich lese den Text und unterstreiche die Wörter, die wichtig sind

und die ich auch aus dem Zusammenhang nicht verstehe.

Unit 5

Outdoor activities

1 **What outdoor activities do these people like? Finish the sentences.**

1 I like _____ .   2 I like _____ .   3 I like _____ .

4 I like _____ .   5 I like _____ .   6 I like _____ .

▶ S. 58

2 **a)** **Look at the class survey.**
Finish the sentences.

Activity		
camping	⊪⊪ II	7
horse riding	III	3
jogging		0
rock climbing	IIII	4
skiing	⊪⊪ IIII	9
swimming	⊪⊪ ⊪⊪ ⊪⊪	15

The most popular outdoor activity is _____ .

Skiing is popular too. _____ pupils like it.

_____ is a popular activity too. Seven

pupils like it. _____ and _____

_____ aren't very popular. Nobody likes

_____ .

b) **What about you? What outdoor activities do you like?**

I like _____

_____

▶ S. 59

3 Which sentence goes with which picture?

1 □ 2 □ 3 □ 4 □ 5 □ 6 □

A Don't forget to take a jacket, good shoes and a map with you when you visit Dartmoor.

B Dartmoor is good for walking, riding and fishing.

C If you need more information, come to our Information Centres. They're open every day.

D Dartmoor rangers can answer all your questions.

E You can see lots of animals on Dartmoor – cows, sheep and ponies.

F Dartmoor is a national park with hills, rivers and woods.

▸ S. 60

4 **a)** Listen again. Tariq's notes about the class trip are wrong.
Correct (= Korrigiere) them.

Trip to Dartmoor – May 13		
9.00	meet at ~~Postbridge~~	school
9.15	leave ~~Information Centre~~	school
10.00	arrive in ~~Harland Tor~~	_____
	visit the ~~school~~	_____
	talk to ~~a picnic~~	_____
	walk to ~~school~~	_____
	have ~~rangers~~	_____
5.00	get back to ~~Dartmoor~~	_____

b) This is Mr Rooney's letter to the parents.
Put in the words from the box.

➡ afternoon • five • food • jacket •
Information • Saturday • shoes • trip

Dear Parents,

On _____ May 13th, we're going on a class _____ to Dartmoor. In the morning we're

visiting the _____ Centre in Postbridge. In the _____ we're walking

to Hartland Tor. Your child needs good _____ , a warm _____ and some _____

for a picnic. We're going to be back at school at _____ o'clock.

Best wishes, Jim Rooney (class teacher)

▸ S. 61

A Day on Dartmoor

5 **a)** Make the right sentences. Draw lines (=*Linien*).

1	In the morning the pupils listened to ...	the weather started to change. **a**
2	Then they walked along a track and saw ...	letter box on Hartland Tor and a stamp. **r**
3	Emma wanted to ...	Serina, a ranger. **t**
4	The class climbed Hartland Tor but ...	she wore a black bag. **s**
5	Emma didn't have a jacket so ...	feed them, but Jamie said no. **e**
6	Later the pupils ...	three more hills and nobody complained. **e**
7	Emma and Sarah found a ...	some ponies. **r**
8	Before lunch they climbed ...	went letterboxing. **u**

b) Fill in the missing word.

1	2	3	4	5	6	7	8
t							

Letterboxing is like a [table] hunt.

▶ S. 63

6 Jamie is writing about the class trip to Dartmoor.
Look at the pictures and finish his text.

In the morning we went to the Information Centre in Postbridge. We looked at lots of

_____ and brochures. Then Serina, a ranger, gave us some rules for

walkers. "Don't feed the _____," she said. "And please stay on

the _____." Later I got a letterboxing _____

and Serina gave me some big black _____ for our litter. We left the Centre.

The track went along a _____ . The weather was nice

and I was the guide for the day. I looked at my map and saw a _____ .

It was Hartland Tor. It was cold now and we could see black _____ .

Emma didn't have her _____ so I gave her a black bag. Everybody

laughed. We climbed three more hills and collected three more _____

for my letterboxing book. It was a great day.

▶ S. 63

WORDPOWER

7 **Good weather or bad weather? Write the weather words in the right boxes.**

→ black clouds • cold • great • nice • rain • sunny • terrible • warm • white clouds

▸S. 64

8 **What are their jobs?**

1 This person drives buses.   *a* _____

2 This person plays football.   _____

3 This person climbs rocks.   _____

4 This person works in a factory.   _____

5 This person sings songs.   _____   ▸S. 64

9 **Look at the words in the box. Put them in the right groups.**

→
- along a river
- climbing
- jacket
- jeans
- riding
- shoes
- through a wood
- up a hill
- walking

Activities	Clothes	Where people go

▸S. 64

10 **What's the odd word out? Say why.**

1 canoeing, horse riding, interesting, rock climbing

" _____ " is the odd word out because it isn't an _____ .

2 children, ponies, pupils, rangers

" _____ " is the odd word out because they aren't _____ .

3 pain, rain, river, sea

" _____ " is the odd word out because it isn't a word for _____ .   ▸S. 64

48

forty-eight

**11 a) Tariq is writing a letter to Mr Rooney.
Put the parts of the letter in the right order.**

☐ Tariq Hassan

☐ July 22nd 2006

☐ Dear Mr Rooney,

☐ Best wishes,

☐ Lakeside View Park, Llangorse Lake, Brecon, Powys, LD3 7TR

☐ PS The postcard shows Cardiff. We were there on Saturday.

☐ I'm on holiday in Wales. I love camping! The weather is great. It's warm and sunny.

☐ Yesterday we climbed a hill and had a picnic there. It was exciting because I found a box with a visitor's book and our school stamp in it!

b) It's July 22nd 2006. Tom is on holiday in Spain. He isn't having fun. Look at the questions and the pictures. Write his letter to Mr Rooney. Tariq's letter can help you.

1 Where's Tom?

2 Does he like camping?

3 What's the weather like?

_____

_____

_____

_____

I'm on holiday in Spain. _____

_____

_____

_____

_____

_____

MUSEUM

4 a) What did he want to do yesterday?

   b) Was it open?

5 Where did they go then?

▶ S. 65

12 **a)** **Read the text and make notes.**

Our class went to Postbridge yesterday. It's a village on Dartmoor. Postbridge is very small but it's nice. The weather was terrible yesterday. It was cold and I didn't have a warm jacket.

Who?	Where?	When?	Description?	Weather?

b) **Read the text and make notes.**

Last summer I had lots of fun. I went to Exmouth with my mum. Exmouth is a town near the sea. It isn't very big, but there are many nice shops and cafes. I had an ice cream every day. The weather was OK. Sometimes it was sunny and sometimes it was cloudy. But it never rained. It was always warm.

Who?	Where?	When?	Description?	Weather?

▶ S. 66

13 **Write about Rebecca's trip. Use the notes.**

Who?	Where?	When?	Description?	Weather?
Rebecca	Neustadt, Germany	last month	small town, near big river, nice people	cold, sunny

▶ S. 66

14 Denise is asking about the new English teacher. What's the best answer? Put a ✔.

1 What does she look like?

☐ Yes, she's friendly.

☐ She's tall.

☐ About 20.

2 How old is she?

☐ I think that's Paula.

☐ She's small.

☐ About 30.

3 And what about her hair?

☐ She has brown hair.

☐ About 40.

☐ She's tall.

4 And is she nice?

☐ Yes, she is.

☐ No, she's friendly.

☐ Yes, she's blonde.   ▸ S. 67

15 Describe Carlo Z. Look at his picture.

What does he look like? _____

How old is he? _____

What about his hair? _____

And is he nice? _____

Carlo Z.
1,51 m
45 years old

▸ S. 67

16 Say it in German. Help an English tourist. He doesn't speak German.
The man at the Information Centre doesn't speak English.

ENGLISH TOURIST

Can you tell me where I can go this afternoon? My favourite outdoor activities are rock climbing and cycling. Can I hire bikes here for my daughter and me? Is it expensive? I think fishing is fun too. Is there a river near here? Tell me, please.

YOU

Er möchte wissen, wohin _____

Seine _____

_____

_____

Außerdem findet er, _____

_____

Das alles würde er gern wissen.   ▸ S. 67

CHECKPOINT

Die Zukunft mit *going to*

Trage hier den Checkpoint aus dem Schülerbuch (Seite 69) ein und schreibe deine eigenen Beispielsätze auf.

Going to benutzt du, um zu sagen, was du vorhast oder dass etwas wahrscheinlich

geschehen wird. Vor *going to* brauchst du _____ .

Nach *going to* steht immer das Verb im _____ , z.B. _____ .

Meine Beispielsätze:

_____

_____

▸ S. 69

17 **Match the sentences to the pictures.
Write 1, 2, … in the boxes.**

1 It's going to be warm but cloudy.

2 It's going to be sunny, but it's going to be cold too.

3 It's going to be cold and cloudy and it's going to rain.

4 It isn't going to rain, but it's going to be cloudy.

A  B

C  D

▸ S. 69

18 **No, that's wrong! Look at the pictures and write what's going to happen.**

1 She's going to play football.

   No! *She's* _____ .

2 They're going to go home by bike.

   No! *They're* _____ .

3 They're going to have a party.

   No! _____

4 He's going to have a hamburger.

   No! _____

▸ S. 69

19 **What are Emily's plans for the weekend? Finish her sentences.**

	✗	✔
Saturday afternoon	help dad	visit Melanie
Saturday evening	read a book	watch TV
Sunday afternoon	write e-mails	do my homework
Sunday evening	watch TV	help dad

1 On Saturday afternoon I'm not going to *help dad*. I'm going to *visit Melanie*.

2 In the evening I'm not going to _____. I'm going to _____.

3 On Sunday afternoon I'm _____.

   I'm _____.

4 In the evening I'm not _____. I'm _____.

▶ S. 69

20 **Rick is going to be in Plymouth next weekend. Paul is talking to him.**
Finish their dialogue. Use *going to* and a verb.

PAUL How long are you going to be in Plymouth, Rick?

RICK We _____ *(be)* there from Friday to Sunday.

PAUL So long? What are you going to do?

RICK Well, on Saturday I _____ *(watch)* a football match with my dad and

   on Sunday morning we _____ *(have)* breakfast in a fast food restaurant.

PAUL And what's your sister going to do?

RICK She's _____ *(stay)* at home.

▶ S. 69

21 **AND YOU? In ten years ... Write two sentences.**

→ be • have • live • work

1 In ten years I'm *going to* _____.

2 In ten years I'm _____.

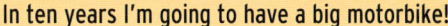
In ten years I'm going to have a big motorbike!

▶ S. 69

1 Find the words.

Cycling Swimming Fishing Skiing Walking camping

1 The Exe is good for _____. There are many fish in it.

2 You need a map when you go _____ on Dartmoor.

3 _____ is my favourite activity. There's a swimming pool near my house.

4 We went _____ last year. It was more exciting than sleeping in a bed!

5 I got a new mountain bike for my birthday. _____ is cool!

6 I don't like _____, because the hills are too high. It's too dangerous.

2 The weather next week. Look at the pictures and write sentences.

1 *On Monday it's going to be* _____.

2 _____

3 _____

MON   TUE   WED

3 Make questions.

look / your / like? / friend / What / does _____

How / this year? / is / old / your friend _____

hair? / What / his / about _____

he / is / And / nice? _____

4 Write sentences with *going to.*

➔ feed the pony • have a picnic •
rain • write a letter

1 It _____.

2 They _____.

3 She _____.

4 He _____.

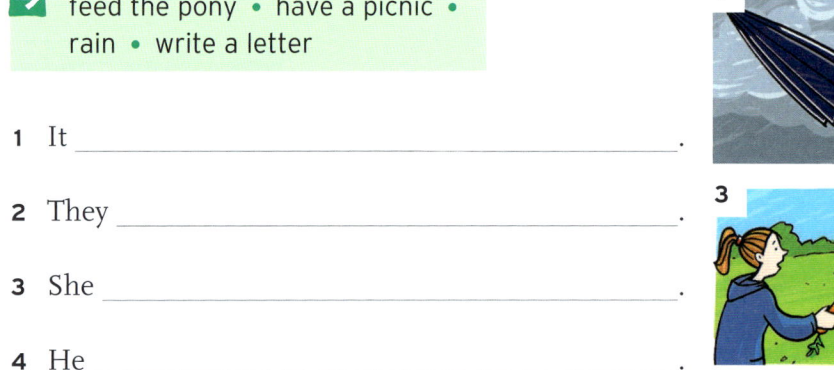

▶ Auf den Seiten 67–68 findest du die Lösungen.

Unit 6

Goodbye to Exeter

1 **a) Listen to the last dialogue again. Then look at this text. Six words are wrong. Underline** *(= Unterstreiche)* **them.**

MAN   Have you ever been to Ireland?

BOY   Yes, I have. It's a boring place. The people are so quiet.

MAN   Where have you been in Ireland?

BOY   I've been everywhere really. My grandma comes from
Belfast and my cousin comes from Dublin, you see.

MAN   So, you've been to the two smallest cities then?

BOY   Oh yes. Very often. They're terrible cities.

b) Now write the right words.

1 _____   3 _____   5 _____

2 _____   4 _____   6 _____

▶ S. 70

2 **Have you ever been to …? Make questions and anwers.**

→ Austria (✘) • Belgium (✔) • France (✔) • Poland (✘) •
the Czech Republic (✔) • the Netherlands (✘)

Yes I have.   No, I haven't.

1 *Have you ever been to Austria?*   – *No, I haven't.*

2 _____   – _____

   _____

3 _____   – _____

   _____

4 _____   – _____

   _____

5 _____   – _____

   _____

6 _____   – _____

   _____

▶ S. 71

Have you ever done this?

3 Finish the sentences with the right words. Put a ✔.

1 Emma, Sarah and Tom went to Jamie's party ...

☐ by car.

☐ by bike.

☐ by train.

2 On the way they stopped at the Turf Cafe and had ...

☐ tea and cake.

☐ orange juice and crisps.

☐ pizza and chips.

3 Next to the railway line they saw ...

☐ an important sign.

☐ a friendly dog.

☐ a cafe.

4 On the other side of the line there was ...

☐ a train.

☐ a small boy.

☐ a cat.

5 Then something very ...

☐ dangerous happened.

☐ different happened.

☐ funny happened.

▶ S. 75

56

fifty-six

4 **a)** Find the end of the sentences. Draw lines (=*Linien*).

1 Tom wanted to open the gate,		he wanted his football. **g**
2 Emma said no,		the train was very near now. **t**
3 The boy on the other side opened the gate,	because	it was too dangerous. **i**
4 Emma ran onto the line,		the boy fell. **h**
5 She picked up the boy and ran back to the others,		he didn't want to wait. **r**

b) What did Tom say about Emma?
Use your answers in a).

1	2	3	4	5

I think Emma did the ⬚⬚⬚⬚⬚ thing.

▶ S. 75

5 **Sarah is writing about Jamie's birthday party. Which words are wrong?**
Underline (= *Unterstreiche*) **them and write the right words.**

1 Tom and I went on the narrow track near the road.

_____

2 We wanted to be funny.

_____

3 After 20 minutes we came to a door next to the railway line.

_____

4 We saw a boy. His football was on the river.

_____

5 He was running across his ball.

_____

6 Emma picked up the boy just after the train came.

_____

▸ S. 76

6 **Pavel can't find his things. Look at the picture and help him.**

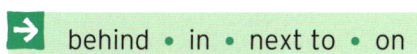 behind • in • next to • on

1 Where's my shoe?   – It's _____ the bed.

2 Where's my exercise book? – It's _____ the cupboard.

3 Where's my jacket?   – It's _____ the bed.

4 Where's my mobile?   – It's _____ the window.

▸ S. 76

7 **Party problems. Use *I'll* ... and the words from the box.**

1 Oh no! We don't have lemonade or cola.

It's OK. I'll go shopping.

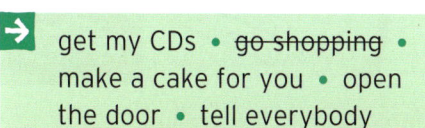 get my CDs • ~~go shopping~~ •
make a cake for you • open
the door • tell everybody

2 Oh no! I forgot to make a cake.

It's OK. _____

3 Oh no! We need music.

_____

4 Oh no! I didn't write invitations.

_____

5 Oh no! Duncan and Sarah are arriving.

_____

▸ S. 76

8 Write Helen's invitation.

In the evening we're going to watch a DVD.

Please come to my birthday party on August 10th.

23 Bridge Street, Plymouth

Helen

Phone: 01752-521850

The party starts at 4 o'clock.

Then we're going to eat pizza.

It finishes at 8 o'clock.

First we're going to go swimming.

▶ S. 77

9 Look at the photos and write Henry's invitation. Helen's invitation can help you.

1

2

3

4

Please come to our _____

First _____

Then _____

In the evening _____

 _____

 _____

_____ Phone: _____

_____

5
Youth Club Party
3-8 o'clock
948 Wood Street, Exeter
Tel: 01392 359826

▶ S. 77

10 Before the party. Lucy is telling her mum what she has just done. Make sentences.

I've just	checked	to the neighbours.
	made	the chairs to my room.
	put	the sandwiches.
	taken	the cake on the table.
	talked	the CDs.

LUCY
I've just checked the CDs.

_____

_____

_____

_____

► S. 78

11 Joshua is going camping with Mike at the weekend. Joshua's dad has questions.

→ Have you taken your mobile phone? • Have you phoned Mike? •
Have you said goodbye to mum? • Have you packed everything?

JOSHUA'S DAD   OK. _____

JOSHUA   Yes, I have. Everything is in my bag.

JOSHUA'S DAD   Good. _____

JOSHUA   Yes, I have. He says he's coming now.

JOSHUA'S DAD   OK. _____

JOSHUA   Yes, I have. It's here. Look.

JOSHUA'S DAD   Good. _____

JOSHUA   No, I haven't. I'll do that now.

► S. 79

12 Say it In German. Help an English friend.

"I've often been to London. But I've never been to Berlin. Is it nice there?"

Er sagt, dass _____

_____

_____

► S. 79

CHECKPOINT

Present perfect

Trage hier den Checkpoint aus dem Schülerbuch (Seite 81) ein und schreibe deine eigenen Beispielsätze auf.

Mit dem *present perfect* sagst du, dass etwas soeben oder schon einmal geschehen ist, z. B.

_____ oder dass etwas (noch) nicht oder (noch) nie geschehen ist, z. B.

_____Du kannst auch fragen,

ob etwas schon einmal geschehen ist: _____

Das *present perfect* bildest du mit _____ oder _____ und einer besonderen Form des Verbs,

dem Partizip Perfekt. Regelmäßige Verben haben die Endung _____,

z. B. _____ .

Einige Verben haben _____ Formen. z. B. _____ .

Meine Beispielsätze:

_____

_____

▶ S. 81

13 **Match the sentences to the pictures.**

➔ • I've often been to Scotland.
• I've just come back from school.
• I've just played tennis.
• I haven't had breakfast.
• Sorry, I haven't done the shopping.
• Have you ever tried canoeing?

1 _____

2 _____

3 _____

4 _____

5 _____

6 _____

▶ S. 81

14 *Have* or *has*? Underline (= *Unterstreiche*) the right word.

1 Catherine isn't talking to me. She *has/have* just had a difficult maths test.

2 Everybody is laughing because mum *have/has* told a funny story.

3 My dad is complaining because I *haven't/hasn't* helped him in the kitchen.

4 *Has/Have* you ever been to France? – No, I *haven't/hasn't*.

5 I'm tired because I*'ve/has* been at school all day.

6 My parents are happy. They *has/'ve* bought a new car.   ▸ S. 81

15 **What are they saying?**

➔ eat • buy • do • take

1 "Jamie! You've _____ my pizza!"

2 "Look! She has _____ my bike!"

3 "Happy Birthday, Jamie!

I've _____ you a present!"

4 "Look! I've _____ all my homework!"   ▸ S. 81

61

sixty-one

16 **AND YOU?** Write sentences with *I've …* or *I've never …*

1 *write / a postcard in English* _____

2 *sit / on a horse* _____

3 *be / jogging* _____

4 *have / my own pet* _____

▸ S. 81

TEST YOURSELF

1 Where has this man been to? Write his sentences.
Use *I've been to ...* or *I've never been to ...*

1 _____

2 _____

3 _____

4 _____

2 What can you see in the picture?

1 _____   4 _____

2 _____   5 _____

3 _____   6 _____

3 It's Cora's birthday. She wants to have a party.
Her friends want to help her. Use *I'll ...*

→ get • make • phone • write

1 KIM _____

2 ANN _____

3 BEN _____

4 ALI _____

the lemonade

a cake

our friends

the invitations

4 Make sentences. Use *I've just ...* and
the right form of the verbs in the box.

→ find • make • phone • take • talk

1 *I've just* _____ David. He says he's coming later.

2 _____ the chairs out of the living room.

3 _____ the salad. Mmm! It's great!

4 _____ my favourite CD. Let's play it.

5 _____ to the neighbours. They think the music is too loud.

▶ Auf der Seite 68 findest du die Lösungen.

Hier kannst du darüber nachdenken, was du in den Units 5 und 6 schon alles gelernt hast.

Das kann ich!

Male die Kästchen aus. Leer bedeutet „das muss ich noch üben" ☐ , halb ausgemalt bedeutet „das kann ich mit Hilfe" ▨ und vollständig ausgemalt bedeutet „das kann ich bereits gut" ▨ .

Unit 5

Ich kann vier Aktivitäten nennen, die man im Freien betreibt.
(Tipp: Schau dir die Übung 1 auf Seite 45 an.) ☐

Ich kann Notizen machen und von einem Ausflug erzählen.
(Tipp: Schau dir die Übung 12 auf Seite 50 an.) ☐

Ich kann in drei Sätzen eine Person beschreiben, z.B. *She is tall.*
(Tipp: Schau dir die Übungen 14 und 15 auf Seite 51 an.) ☐

Ich kann drei Sätze über das Wetter in den nächsten Tagen bilden,
z.B. *It's going to be warm.*
(Tipp: Schau dir die Übung 17 auf Seite 52 an.) ☐

Ich kann in fünf Sätzen über meine Pläne sprechen, z.B. *I'm going to ...*
(Tipp: Schau dir die Übungen 19–21 auf Seite 53 an.) ☐

Meine schön gestaltete Arbeit. Der Titel meiner Arbeit für mein Portfolio lautet:

Unit 6

Ich kann fragen, wo jemand schon gewesen ist.
(Tipp: Schau dir die Übung 2 auf Seite 55 an.) ☐

Ich kann fünf von Deutschlands Nachbarländern nennen.
(Tipp: Schau dir die Übung 2 auf Seite 55 an.) ☐

Ich kann vier Sätze bilden, in denen ich jemandem spontan Hilfe anbiete.
(Tipp: Schau dir die Übung 7 auf Seite 57 an.) ☐

Ich kann eine Einladungskarte schreiben.
(Tipp: Schau dir die Übung 9 und 10 auf Seite 58 an.) ☐

Ich kann sagen, was gerade passiert ist.
(Tipp: Schau dir die Übung 11 auf Seite 59 an.) ☐

Ich kann in vier Sätzen sagen, was noch nie geschehen ist.
(Tipp: Schau dir die Übung 16 auf Seite 61 an.) ☐

Meine schön gestaltete Arbeit. Der Titel meiner Arbeit für mein Portfolio lautet:

Tipp: Du kannst auch deine Lehrerin / deinen Lehrer fragen,
welche Fortschritte du im Englischunterricht gemacht hast.

PORTFOLIO

Das kann ich auch noch!

Ich kann fünf Sportarten nennen.
(Tipp: Schau dir Seite 59 im Schülerbuch 2 an.)

Ich kann auf Englisch bis hundert zählen.
(Tipp: Schau dir Seite 167 im Schülerbuch 2 an.)

Ready for *New Highlight 3!*

Band 2 von *New Highlight* hast du fast geschafft. Prima! Lies dir die folgenden Fertigkeiten durch. Beherrschst du sie schon gut ☺? Beherrschst du sie nur mittelmäßig 😐? Oder hast du das Gefühl, dass du sie noch gar nicht kannst ☹? Hake ab.

Ich kann:	☺	😐	☹
… verstehen, was meine Lehrerin sagt.			
… verstehen, wenn sie eine Geschichte vorliest.			
… verstehen, wenn ich die Geschichte von der CD höre.			
… längere Texte (z.B. *stories*) lesen und verstehen.			
… neue Wörter in einem Text verstehen.			
… das Wörterverzeichnis (Seite 147–166) schnell benutzen.			
… mit den *Checkpoints* gut umgehen.			
… bei Partner- und Gruppenarbeit mitmachen.			
… meine Hausaufgaben selbstständig erledigen.			
… fragen, wenn ich etwas nicht verstanden habe.			
… mir selbstständig helfen, wenn ich etwas nicht verstanden habe.			

Quiz

Wie gut kennst du Sarah, Jamie, Emma und Tom und die Klasse 8R?
Unterstreiche die richtige Antwort.

UNIT 1 Where's Tariq from? *Scotland/Somalia/Spain*

UNIT 2 Who's Tom's cousin? *Jane/Jenny/Jutta*

UNIT 3 What's the name of Mr Johnson's restaurant? *The Sea / The Sun / The Surprise*

UNIT 4 What did Emma and Sally take from Debenhams? *CDs/Jeans/T-shirts*

UNIT 5 Where did Class 8R go on a school trip? *To a city / To a museum / To a national park*

UNIT 6 What did Jamie have at the end of July? *A birthday party / A goodbye party / A welcome party*

Wenn du Probleme bei der Punktevergabe hast, bitte deine Lehrerin / deinen Lehrer um Hilfe.

Unit 1

1 Make five more words.

2 *exercise book*   5 *pencil case*
3 *football match*   6 *town centre*
4 *homework diary*

Gib dir für jedes richtig zugeordnete Wort 0,5 Punkte. Deine Punktzahl:

2 Which word isn't right?

1 *uniform*   4 *lunch*
2 *rubber*   5 *brochure*
3 *playground*   6 *meet*

Gib dir für jedes richtige Wort 0,5 Punkte. Deine Punktzahl:

3 Make sentences for the pictures.

2 *Don't eat* in the classroom, please.
3 *Don't talk, please.*
4 *Open/Close* the window, please.

Gib dir für jeden richtigen Satz 2 Punkte. Deine Punktzahl:

4 What can you say?

1 Sorry. I'*m using* it.
2 I'*m not eating.*
3 Sorry. I'*m meeting* my mother after school.
4 Yes, they are. But they'*re feeling* tired.

Gib dir für jede richtige Lösung 1 Punkt. Deine Punktzahl:

**Zähle alle Punkte zusammen.
Von insgesamt 15,5 Punkten
hast du erreicht:**

TESTERGEBNIS

15,5 – 14 Punkte:
Du bist richtig fit in Englisch. Mache weiter so!

13,5 – 11,5 Punkte:
Deine Englischkenntnisse sind gut. Versuche die kleinen Fehler noch zu vermeiden.

11 – 8,5 Punkte:
Du kannst schon recht gut Englisch. Aber: du musst noch genauer lernen, um besser zu werden.

8 – 6 Punkte:
Du kannst einiges in Englisch. Leider hast du noch einige Lücken. Frage deine Lehrerin / deinen Lehrer, wie du diese Lücken schließen kannst.

5,5 – 0 Punkte:
Leider hat es dieses Mal nicht so gut geklappt. Du hast noch erhebliche Lücken. Frage deine Lehrerin / deinen Lehrer, wie du diese Lücken schließen kannst.

UNIT 2

1 Make eight words.

1 *cousin*   4 *passage*   7 *visitor*
2 *kilometre*   5 *singer*   8 *water*
3 *mobile*   6 *tunnel*

Gib dir für jedes richtig zugeordnete Wort 0,5 Punkte. Deine Punktzahl:

2 Which is the right sentence?

a) *1*   b) *1*

Gib dir für jeden richtigen Satz 0,5 Punkte. Deine Punktzahl:

3 Put the sentences together ...

2 *I like it. Everybody is very nice.*
3 *It's great. I like English breakfasts.*
4 *Can I have a glass of milk instead of tea?*
5 *OK. But I miss my mum and dad.*

Gib dir für jede richtige Lösung 1 Punkt. Deine Punktzahl:

* Bei der Bewertung der Übungen mit Punkten wurde in der Regel nach folgenden Kriterien vorgegangen: Für ein Lösungswort, das nur zugeordnet werden muss, gibt es 0,5 Punkte. Bei einem selbstständig zu schreibenden Lösungswort oder einem Satz, der nur zugeordnet werden muss, 1 Punkt, bei der selbstständigen Formulierung eines ganzen Satzes 2 Punkte.

4 Make the questions.
1 What's *more expensive* than tea?
2 What's *cheaper* than mineral water?
3 What's the *most expensive* drink?
4 What's the *cheapest* drink?

Gib dir für jede richtige Lösung 1 Punkt.
Deine Punktzahl:

Zähle alle Punkte zusammen.
Von insgesamt 13 Punkten
hast du erreicht:

UNIT 3

1 What are the jobs?
1 *baggage handler(s)*   4 *security guard*
2 *bus driver*   5 *shop assistant*
3 *police officer(s)*   6 *sports teacher*

Gib dir für jede richtige Lösung 1 Punkt.
Deine Punktzahl:

2 Put in *was* or *were*.
1 I *was* tired.
2 You *were* right.
3 There *were* no jobs in London.
4 It *was* her dream job.

Gib dir für jede richtige Lösung 1 Punkt.
Deine Punktzahl:

3 Finish the sentences.
1 He *had* no job and he was unhappy.
2 She *made* a salad roll for me.
3 I *saw* you with your dad in a cafe.
4 She *went* to the bank ...
5 We *had* fish and chips for lunch.
6 They *looked* at the new ...

Gib dir für jedes richtige Wort 1 Punkt.
Deine Punktzahl:

4 Make the dialogue.
SARAH Hi, Emma! How *was* your weekend?
EMMA   *Fine.* I went to the *cinema.*
       We *watched* a great film.
       What about you?
SARAH Oh, I fell off a *horse.*
EMMA   *Poor you!* Are you OK?
SARAH *No, I'm not.* I hurt my arm. I can't
       go to school *tomorrow.*

Gib dir für jede richtige Lösung 0,5
Punkte. Deine Punktzahl:

Zähle alle Punkte zusammen.
Von insgesamt 20,5 Punkten
hast du erreicht:

UNIT 4

1 It's Monday afternoon.

1 I wouldn't like *to go shopping.*
2 *I'd like to watch TV.*
3 *I'd like to eat an ice cream.*
4 *I wouldn't like to play alone.*

Gib dir für jeden richtigen Satz 1 Punkt.
Deine Punktzahl:

2 Make six words.

2 *girlfriend*   5 *sometimes*
3 *newspaper*   6 *weekend*
4 *shoplifter*

Gib dir für jedes richtige Wort 0,5 Punkte.
Deine Punktzahl:

3 What the Lees didn't do …

1 *Mr Lee didn't go shopping.*
2 *Mrs Lee didn't watch TV.*
3 *David didn't read his new book.*

Gib dir für jede richtige Lösung 1 Punkt.
Deine Punktzahl:

4 In the evening …

2 DAD   *Did you visit / play a game with*
              grandma?
   JOSH Yes, *I did.*
3 DAD   *Did you do your* homework?
   JOSH *No, I didn't.*
4 DAD   *Did you buy a present for* mum?
   JOSH *Yes, I did.*

Gib dir für richtige Frage 2 Punkte, für
jede richtige Antwort 1 Punkt.
Deine Punktzahl:

Zähle alle Punkte zusammen.
Von insgesamt 18,5 Punkten
hast du erreicht:

UNIT 5

1 Find the words.

1 The Exe is good for *fishing.*
2 You need a map when you go *walking* …
3 *Swimming* is my favourite activity …
4 We went *camping* last year.
5 *Cycling* is cool!
6 I don't like *skiing* because the hills are
   too high.

Gib dir für jedes richtige Wort 0,5 Punkte.
Deine Punktzahl:

2 The weather next week

1 On Monday it's going to be *cold and*
   sunny.
2 *On Tuesday it's going to be warm.*
3 *On Wednesday it's going to be cloudy.*

Gib dir für jeden richtigen Satz 2 Punkte.
Deine Punktzahl:

3 Make questions.

1 *What does your friend look like?*
2 *How old is your friend this year?*
3 *What about his hair?*
4 *And is he nice?*

Gib dir für jede richtige Lösung 1 Punkt.
Deine Punktzahl:

4 **Write sentences with *going to*.**
1 It*'s going to rain.*
2 She*'s going to feed the pony.*
3 They*'re going to have a picnic.*
4 He*'s going to write a letter.*

Gib dir für jeden richtigen Satz 2 Punkte.
Deine Punktzahl:

Zähle alle Punkte zusammen.
Von insgesamt 21 Punkten hast du
erreicht:

UNIT 6

1 **Where has this man been to?**
1 I*'ve been to Ireland.*
2 I*'ve never been to Austria.*
3 I*'ve been to Switzerland.*
4 I*'ve been to Poland.*

Gib dir für jede richtig Lösung 1 Punkt.
Deine Punktzahl:

2 **What can you see in the picture?**
1 *train*   4 *railway line*
2 *bridge*   5 *car*
3 *canal*   6 *hotel*

Gib dir für jedes richtige Wort 0,5 Punkte.
Deine Punktzahl:

3 **It's Cora's birthday.**
1 I*'ll get the lemonade.*
2 I*'ll make a cake.*
3 I*'ll phone our friends.*
4 I*'ll write the invitations.*

Gib dir für jeden richtigen Satz 1 Punkt.
Deine Punktzahl:

4 **Make sentences.**
1 I*'ve just phoned* David.
2 I*'ve just taken* the chairs out of the
   living room.
3 I*'ve just made* the salad.
4 I*'ve just found* my favourite CD.
5 I*'ve just talked* to the neighbours.

Gib dir für jede richtige Lösung 1 Punkt.
Deine Punktzahl:

Zähle alle Punkte zusammen.
Von insgesamt 16 Punkten hast du
erreicht: